THE GLORY OF GLORIES

Dominick Mereworth

Foreword
By
Professor Suheil Bushrui

ARCTURUS PRESS

2005

ISBN 0 907322 97 2

Published by

Arcturus Press
The Manse : Fleet Hargate : Lincolnshire PE12 8LL
Phone 01406 423971 : Fax 01406 422191

CONTENTS

FOREWORD
by
SUHElL BUSHRUI

Bahai Chair for World Peace
Center for International Development and
Conflict Management
University of Maryland, USA.

God and Soul are words that are not fashionable in a world that is dissociating itself from its spiritual roots, hiding its emptiness behind walls of materialism. Yet we can never escape from what is within us; however deeply buried, the soul of man remains. If we are ever to advance towards a global Society, it is our soul that must be revitalized. And it is to the poet that we look for hope. Throughout history, the poet has never ceased in his quest to arouse the spirit of Truth, the God in all men.

   The poetry of Dominick Mereworth is inspired by profoundly spiritual faith. This collection of poems, The Glory of Glories, powerfully expresses promptings of the soul. In his poetry he has allowed the sun to touch the mirror of his soul and we look at the mirror 'to see the God within'. Although the foundation of Dominick Mereworth's faith is Bahai, he leaves us in no doubt that the awareness of God Almighty, the Creator of all, is universal in every sense of the word. Dominick Mereworth speaks as a poet, and because he speaks as a poet, he speaks of God to the soul of all men.

Suheil Bushrui
May 2005

INTRODUCTION
AND
ACKNOWLEDGEMENTS

The Glory of Glories is a humble expression of the light, knowledge and wisdom received from the teachings and writings of the Founders of the Bahá'i Faith, The Báb and Bahá'u'lláh, also His son Abdu'l Bahá.

I was introduced to the Bahá'i Faith in Dublin by the American actor O. Z. Whitehead, who was also an author of books on the Faith. After becoming a follower of Bahá'u'lláh my life changed and the nucleus understanding I had of the Creator and the world was transformed.

I was most fortunate in that I was taught and guided by some of the most knowledgeable members of the Bahá'i Faith, notably the late Adib Taherzadeh, a former member of the Universal House of Justice, and his wife Lesley; Doris Holley, widow of the Hand of the Cause of God, Horace Holley and the late David Hofman, a former member of the Universal House of Justice, whose book on The Hand of the Cause George Townshend I helped in a small way to research.

Professor Suheil Bushrui, a scholar of international repute as a translator and interpreter of Anglo-Irish literature to the Arab world and the author of critical studies in both Arabic and English on W.B. Yeats, J.M. Synge, James Joyce and Samuel Beckett, has greatly honoured me by writing the Foreword to this book.

When I left Ireland and returned to London in 1987, I was made most welcome by the Secretary of the National Spiritual Assembly, Hugh Adamson and his wife Lynda, and also by the members of the Bahá'i Community of Kensington & Chelsea and the local Assembly. Since then, I have made so many friends and received so much kindness from so many people that it is impossible to name them all here, but at the risk of seeming invidious I feel that I must make special mention of the following who have particularly helped and encouraged me in my poetical endeavours and pray that any inadvertent omissions will be treated charitably.

So (in no particular order) to Dr Foadi, Reza Jahangiri, Surat Bayat, Nabil Khodadad, the Djalili family, Maryam Nousha and Samandar Samari, Lady Lilian Carpenter, and special thanks to Shamsi Navidi and family, Graham and Guilda Walker, Vafa and Tamineh Payman, Tanaz Atlassi and family and all the Westminster Assembly and Community, Iqbal and Nasrin Latif, Farjad Farid (Founder of World Citizenship), Walter Martindale, John Mathews and family, Hilary Freeman, Bunny Evans, Mr and Mrs Alaee, Keyvan Aghai, Vasa Ram, Darshan and Nergez Manocha, Nora Evans, the Gibraltar Assembly and Community, and last but not least, Dermod Knox, who has always supported my poetical endeavours and has advised me on this book, I send my warmest thanks and best wishes.

Finally, Peter Erwood, proprietor of Arcturus Press, the publishers of this volume, though not of the Bahá'í Faith himself, was once the chief assistant to the late David Hofman (see above) who published a number of Bahá'í books during the late 1950s and early 1960s. Such a coincidence, unknown to me when I first approached Arcturus Press, has proved to be most beneficial.

Dominick Mereworth
May 2005.

DOMINICK MEREWORTH

Dominick Mereworth, the chairman of Oranmore Productions Ltd, is variously a playwright, poet, theatrical entrepreneur - and hereditary peer. His past business undertakings include agriculture, public relations and ownership of a coffee bar/restaurant.

Previous works for the stage have been produced on the London fringe and in Belfast and Cork, notably : *I, Mary Magdalene* (three productions); *Family Rules*; *Cast off the Veil*; *Seal of Rome*; *Stoned*, and *The Moment Came*. Several other works are now ready for development for stage purposes.

Dominick has also written a film script *Golden Head*, based on the Irish legend of Niamh and Olsin. He contributed a chapter *Exiles: A Moral Statement*, to *James Joyce - An International Perspective*. (Irish Literary Studies, 10 - 1982)

Two past volumes of poetry, *Poems* and *Bestowals* are now followed by the present volume, *Glory of Glories*, with *The Sparkling Fountain*, to be published shortly by Arcturus Press.

Dominick has extensive commitments in the voluntary sector - notable as Patron, Kent Refugee Action Network; President, Celtic Vision; and Vice-President, Veterans in Europe/Monte Cassino Federation for Remembrance and Reconciliation.

Richard C. Wassell
April 2005

I

THE BIRTH OF THE BÁB

Oh, Holiness The Báb
  You are the gateway to life,
  humankind distraught with strife.
  You lead us from the dark wood,
  Our hearts blinded with a hood,
  To the glorious eternal light.
  Bahá'u'lláh,
  The glory of the Creator stood,
  world unity where justice serves,
  love and finally peace
  to all life on this earth.

The Báb, this crown, this gateway,
  This mouthpiece from the Creator,
  Introducing the opening
  To the new Kingdom, this day
  born of substance, not of this clay,
  but destined the foundation
  of this glorious age to lay.
  A spiritual history, a creation
  Of a new man, evolved transformed
  Through suffering's horrific rage,
  Human abasement, forlorn.

His Holiness The Báb's shrine
   On the mount of The Lord,
   Carmel, stands the Queen of all,
   An edifice with a diadem of gold,
   Rising from the earth,
   To the fine supreme spiritual birth.
   This monument glows splendidly
   scintillating, stands out resplendently
   a pinnacle of gold, a crown
   viewed from the bay of Haifa
   for all the world a shrine renowned.

II

THE BÁB

Mouthpiece from the Creator
representing the inception
to the New Kingdom this day.
Born of substance, not of this clay,
but destined to lay the foundation
of this glorious epoch,
a spiritual history, a creation.

III

THE BÁBÍ ERA

Why did you die without fear?
  Why did you suffer
  without a tear?
  From red-hot burns
  and dreadful spears?
  Twenty thousand Persians,
  blood flowing in the streets,
  twenty thousand tortured
  for this new life's way,
  of His Holiness The Báb
  on this glorious day.

During those nine horrific,
  splendid years of tears,
  civilization advanced more
  than many millenniums in years.
  From the innocence
  of that bloodstained earth
  grows this wonderful plant,
  this new world order, worth
  more than all, that life has past
  flowering into red roses,
  perfume exquisite, passionate thirst
  for justice to produce the birth
  of love and peace on this earth.

IV

RIDVÁN 21st APRIL

Raindrops of tears, sprinkling
    from the balconies and rooftops
    of Baghdad, joining the river Tigris,
    an overflowing stream
    of sorrow, never ceased.

He, the glory of glories,
    from a boat,
    departing, spoke:

"I entrust to your keeping
    this city of Baghdad...
    With you
    it now rests to watch,
    lest your deeds and conduct
    dim the flame of love
    that gloweth within the breasts
    of its inhabitants."*

As the Muezzin raised
    the prayerful note,
    Bahá'u'lláh was praised.

*God Passes By, p.149

Entering the garden of delight,
    by His grace the world awoke
    and forgiveness He blazed
    as the horizon bright.

A new creation of humankind
    from His word sublime He spoke,
    unfolded, stirred, dazed,
    from His origin, again awoke.

V

THE BIRTH OF BAHÁ'U'LLÁH

Beyond the misty hue the dawn.
   Awake, awake, the great day is born.
   It is not the hour for souls to sleep.
   Awake, awake, an early vigil keep.

Every atom is struck; all life has grown
   Because The Blessed Beauty
   His glory has shown.
   The sun has risen before
   on many a day,
   But never before shown
   with such a stupendous ray.

All life in abundance has come this dawn
   As the Father of all mankind is born.

VI

BEFORE A BAHÁ'I FEAST

The waiting for the song,
   the song, the melody,
   the music from the soul
   to sing, to sing,
   holy words to become a rhapsody.

The talk, after one guest
   arrives, another, waiting
   for the melody, the song,
   to sing, to sing,
   holy words to become a rhapsody.

The hostess gives tea,
   biscuits and sweet love,
   for the melody, the song,
   to sing, to sing,
   holy words to give rhapsody.

The atmosphere imbibes,
   the talk, the talk, waiting
   for the melody, the melody
   to sing, to sing,
   holy words to give rhapsody.

The chairperson speaks,
    welcomes, thanking the hostess
    for the melody, the melody
    to sing, to sing,
    holy words to give rhapsody.

Silence, not a word to speak,
    backs straighten, feet meet
    for the melody, the melody,
    to sing, to sing,
    holy words give rhapsody.

GLORY OF GLORIES

When Bahá'u'lláh His glory
appeared, whispering grass
played the tuneful story,
that out of the root of old
that tree of destiny would unfold.
The most glorious vision
Ever on this earth to be told.

This vision is paradise sealed,
proclaiming the voice of the Lord
one day would be revealed
prophesied by the prophets of old.
That the face of the Lord
On this earth we would be seeing,
Bringing happiness, taking
Away all afflicted feelings.

VIII

THE SPIRITUAL SUN

Every day the sunlight appears.
It brings growth and life
to our sphere,
the light dazzling, strong is
our wealth
without it, humankind
would be without health.

The sun comes up every day,
dries the grass into hay.
It also gives us time to play,
Beethoven, Mozart, Shakespeare.
If the sun did not return,
how could we live or learn?

Is it enough for us to love,
on material life to be fed;
can we live only on bread?
Another sun, more powerful still,
unseen behind the daffodil
has power to change our life,
so that we can grow to be free,
be part of the spiritual tree.

If every day were a thousand years
   or more, the sun would still appear
   bringing material and spiritual form.
   The spiritual Word is the messenger
   of God
   Buddha, Moses, Christ, Muhammad
   For this day Bahá'ulláh, bringing
   life to the soil, feeding the corn,
   awakening teachings for the dawn,
   taking the world from ignorant night
   to the greatest potency of light.

IX

THE RESULT OF RIDVÁN

On this earth darkness was shorn,
  clouds dispersed, a vision,
  a dream, millions believe was born.
  The light, bright, brings decisions,
  as unity filled with Justice bursts.
  Bahá'ulláh, the spiritual sun,
  has risen.

This day ignorance has ceased.
    People are able to speak peace;
    their heads think justice; their lips
    with love the cup do sip.
    Men and women happily dance
    a tune of joy; the heart dips.
    Bahá'u'lláh with his creative word
    speaks forth, divinely lifts
    humankind from the bed of silt
    to the height of the eternal gift.

X

NO SECRET

Why do you whisper?
   There is no secret now.
   .All is revealed since
   the passing of 'Abdu'l-Bahá.

The Father revealed all;
   The Son interpreted the script.
   Why worry? It has all been explained
   now, through the Master's lips.

XI

RIDVAN
ON ENTERING THE GARDEN
OF PARADISE

Bahá'u'lláh, the Glory of Glories,
  before embarking on a boat,
  words of love and encouragement
  spoke.

From balconies and rooftops
  of Baghdad, tears of raindrops
  flow into the river Tigris
  stream of human sorrow
  never ends.

On entering The Garden of Paradise,
  the muezzin prayerful notes were raised
  beyond the clouds, the sun of delight,
  the chant for Bahá'u'lláh was praised.

Through the clear space, His light,
  His vision, shook with fire ablaze.
  All humankind with one stroke
  Was changed. He forgave.

He who had hidden His Face
    had now come with infinite grace.
    of a new man, evolved transformed
    through suffering horrific,
    human abasement, forlorn.

XII

THE NEW TREE

What is this sun
    clothed with rays of life
    that scorched the seed,
    developing the new tree
    that gives the air
    for man to breathe ...

What is this sun
    that gives us life?
    These rays that
    nurture the smallest mite,
    the bean seeds
    that harvest ripe.

That glorious sun
    of the Holy Spirit
    involved with rays
    which beneath all this glory lay
    the abundance of
    His precious day.

XIII

PRAYERS TO BE ANSWERED

So pure and so strong
   through his wisdom
   he seldom did wrong.
   His kindness was sublime,
   he gave to all mankind.

You could be sure
   His prayers would be heard,
   from his heart they were
   sincere.

Yet to be answered
   that is a call of spiritual justice
   from the Lord of the Spheres.

XIV

THE SEA STORY

In the sea there is a story
the waves foretell, the rhythm
beating against the cliffs.
History calls us,
calls us from our ancient stock,
unfolding the destiny of our future,
the unknown water, against the rock
rolling, crashing to the glory
of Bahá'u'lláh's new world order.

The shape of colours and molecules,
the shining light with sparkling hues,
to our destiny sea waves
will shock us,
breaking up against the rocks,
destroying all the rubbish,
cleansing all that comes across us,
sifting all dogma from the glory,
showing us in heavenly order
to be the dwellers in
The New World.

What can you say about this story?
  Is it full of problems for us?
  Will the sea come in to devour us?
  Will the waves cascade
  and drown us?
  Or will the glory of the Lord triumph,
  sweeping aside all
  that in the past has destroyed us.

XV

THE CELEBRATION OF NAW-RÚZ

The Fast was a blessing; it is
    given with love by Bahá'u'lláh.
    His revealed prayers said more
    than on your fingers you could count,
    with precious loving gifts
    from the ever-flowing
    divine fount.

The suffering, if it was impaled,
    reminds us of the
    Blessed beauty.
    His pain numbered without fail
    more than we could bear
    The bastinado!
    The monsters, how could
    they dare!

The Fast is finally finished,
    Naw-Rúz has begun.
    Ring the bells,
    let's all join in the fun.

But now, because of His pain,
   we can sing, dance and claim
   the Lord of the Kingdom came
   in His Majesty once again.
   so link your arms in unity
   because of the
   Blessed Perfection.
   Now live in purest amity.

So take up your cups,
   link your arms and kiss.
   Because of the Blessed Perfect,
   now live in heavenly bliss.

XVI

THE BEGINNING OF THE NEW WORLD ORDER

Shadows filled the space,
   complete darkness overshadowed
all around in every place.
Thunder roared.
Across the pitch blackness
lightning soared.
Through the crevice
of that obscurity
death fell from the sky;
human lungs polluted,
carnage piled high.

Why had the end come
   with such a pool of mud?
As the earth's surface
collapsed with a sudden thud.
Out of the world had come
spreading madness.
A sudden outburst of hatred
pervaded the world with sadness.
The blackness continued
to devastate the earth.
Life was threatened
through lack of human worth.

XVII

THE MYSTERY OF THE CREATOR

The enigma of the Universe
a tapestry in colours, purple, white,
and in your head, with threads
unknown, woven by its Creator
,fashioned by the mysterious word
"read".

Its spiritual power through man's
mind enhances his chance from his
Maker forever to bring an ever
advancing civilization, along with
the command to find and worship
that Creator.

For always has the Unknown shown His
wisdom, power, through His words
spiritual hearing, divine in laws,
moral educational worth, to taste,
digest and assuage yearning
revealed by the mouth of
The Manifestation, human in form,
divine in spiritual therapy.

The divine shining through
   The Manifestation.
   God, the Beauty is seen in
   His beauty and in His Being,
   but His Being; and in His Self,
   but His Self; and in His movement,
   but His movement; and
   in His acquiescence
   but His acquiescence;
   and in His pen but His pen.

The Mighty, the All Praised,
   there hath not been in His Soul,
   but the Truth and Himself.
   Naught can be seen but God
   through the temple of
   The Manifestation.
   Except for this, the Secret never
   solved,

The Unknown, still unknown, hidden
   in His-Her-Its mystery, without
   formation,
   only by Divine Revelation known,
   concealed in no way revealed.

Imagination can in no way conceive
    the divine grown, in conception
    outside all attributes, any seed, or
    concept, even above any name or any
    need.

In fact if any idol is made in the mind,
    or chain of events of the eternal
    divine
    or stone edifice of gross design,
    these concepts are restricting
    the eternal which is limitless,
    unthinkable, immortal, Divine,
    all-encompassing without confine,
    shape, colour, imagination of any
    size, cannot fit into the brain,
    a terminal resign.

So where are you, Eternal Mystery?
    For God's sake show Thy face,
    uncover Thy veil, so that humankind
    may come to know his Creator;
    hence know His Self,
    and out of His Soul, hail!
    with extreme praise and
    acknowledge the source
    Of all life and existence.

His power never fails to reach humankind,
  His exalted position, His course,
  His manifestation, through His
  mouthpiece for the day,
  His prophet supreme, exalted by
  His extreme glory.

His magnificent all ascending face is seen.
  It sends the Holy Spirit like the sun
  its rays to the poverty of humankind
  suffering story,
  to lift him up to taste his Lord's
  glory.

And man, "Noble have I created thee
  I have created within thee,
  a breath of my own spirit"
  alive, dancing, prancing, with joy
  but this spirit must be made true
  awakened by the word of
  the Manifestation revealed through
  the Creator's new message to His
  creation, clarification, light ablaze,
  and knowledge scaled to a height,
  a peak never before reached, of toil
  and spiritual government founded
  in a world new and completely
  grounded in truth, reality and justice.

XVIII

THE NEW AGE

The moon gapes in hope.
    A reflection of the sun in glass,
    shades all the corruption
    during the days of destruction.

A new age beats upon the earth,
    the vibrations from man's
    endeavours through divine
    intervention, his worth.
    His aspirations vent
    the desires from his heart
    to his breast, lent
    strong blood from his veins.
    to remould the whole part
    with an enlightened brain.

To re-sculpture man,
    from a cast iron heart,
    an edifice, with a cold start
    to an embodiment of warm
    breathing new succulent air
    flowing compassion, justice
    born from the cocoon of despair.

This image of new man,
　　his sincerity will not be spared,
　　his attraction, a magnet to a metal.
　　Whatever craft cannot stand apart,
　　his faithfulness and love.
　　Truthfulness from his heart
　　loving kindness to all people.
　　This global furnace of fire,
　　will be transfixed by a sweet
　　song, that all the souls
　　in the vast heavens will meet
　　for the birth of this changed
　　sphere, truthfulness not to cheat
　　on this earth, The Creator's seat.

XIX

THE TRUTH SATISFIES THE SOUL

Why is it a person
    so kind and mature,
    advanced in years
    lives so graciously
    and worldly wise is sure?
    She gives up her time
    to be with you apart
    even though she works
    from dawn to dusk
    to spread the cheese
    put butter on the crust.

Why is it then,
    when she is so apparently
    so very sincere,
    her intelligence is bright
    and is certainly able to hear?
    What is that prevents
    the growth of her evolving soul
    holding the person, in fear,
    from recognizing the truth,
    thus born of the spirit
    making a fresh new youth.

Is she clinging to tradition
   through the leaders of religion?
   The ideas of her forefathers,
   veiling, hiding her vision,
   drowning her in a mire of lather,
   from an ancient old-world mission,
   rather than the fresh spring
   with a magnate live creation
   of Bahá'u'lláh's ever
   advancing civilization.

XX

WORLD CITIZENSHIP

Do you belong to the world?
　　The one and same human race
　　with all the varied people,
　　each with a different face.
　　These people are all like
　　the same part of one nucleus,
　　protons and neutrons,
　　spread over the world
　　with a different chance
　　of destruction or surviving,
　　chance of living or dying.

Down under the sky
　　that rings the globe
　　away from the tortured cry
　　world citizens begin
　　to recognize and know,
　　that their existence below
　　must be unity for the whole,
　　not the prison of uniformity
　　yet the difference of variety,
　　which shapes the art,
　　The colour, not the life stark.

This leaves countries free
for national autonomy
and cultural diversity.

World citizenship embraces amity,
Nobility and human dignity.
Joining trust with loyalty,
consultation, making decisions,
disagreements without derision,
leaving people in lovable unity,
for advancement of the community.

XXI

THE LIGHT OF JUSTICE

The light means understanding
   the knowledge that has come,
   no more in the black pit
   of ignorance,
   now we can see the sun.

The sun resembles Bahá'u'lláh.
   Light and love he brings
   from that wealth of heat.
   We know evolution sings
   of how life has sprung
   towards knowledge of
   the opera of unity with love,
   where understanding is sung.

And from that unity
   justice was born.
   What an exalted word
   on the strings
   of the heart to be worn.

If justice existed
   between man and man,
   we could follow a united plan.
   The Creator has given
   one pillar for reward
   and one for punishment;
   also in between
   for safety's sake,
   he has given His bounty
   to all the human race,
   forgiveness, through His grace.

XXII

THE RIDVÁN ISLE OF WIGHT

A call from the past, trepidation cast,
as the voice of enthusiasm, direct.
Love for Bahá'u'lláh came from
the organizer, the leader inspired,
kind, strong, organized, designed,
generous, rare to find.
A team he organized in unity, love.

XXIII

JUSTICE BRINGS PEACE

Peace is an inevitable cause,
    can be proved as long as human kind
    understands the reason laws,
    that the whole world must
    have in mind
    peace, but justice is the reason sure,
    that brings global peace to
    every shore.

Justice is the only peaceful elite
    without it love will not stand
    complete.
    Peace is not a game played
    on a board
    or a placard carried high with
    a reward
    for in every limb; and complex cell
    justice in red blood, humanity
    must spell.

This world must practice justice,
    for with justice a star stands bright
    love without justice is the sun
    without light.

From the sun's rays justice shines,
  a beam of star filled light,
  love gives growth, justice a sweet wine.
  Without justice, imbalance occurs,
  brains topple as they become
  confused with drastic ugly curves.

XXIV

FROM SORROW TO JOY

Rejoice in your sorrow
  For joy may come to morrow
  Rejoice for out of sadness
  Comes the fountain of happiness
  from the misery of this natural strife
  Grows the soul of everlasting life.

When the heartache comes
  too much to take
  and the physical pain at night awake
  Rejoice, rejoice.
  Life from the cage the bird is freed.
  Can fly high up to grasp all need.
  But we want to live now, and free
  on this earth, mother nature let us be.

Nature is bound by rule and ground,
   like the rose it has no means
   to float around.
   To prune it for growth will encourage
   its beauty,
   cause it to bleed and steady the
   bloom for its duty
   to serve humanity, that is every sort
   and kind
   no distinction between the visionary
    and the blind
   for the blind can see only an ocean
   so green.

The visionary knows where to sow the seed,
   that flourishes amongst the most
   pernicious weed.

XXV

THE HUMAN BODY IN UNITY

The human heart follows Nature's pattern.
   The limbs and the toes join in one
   caption,
   From the head to the feet in unity
   meet
   One whole creation, God's Holy Seat.

The stars in the sky in unison greet,
   The world in one unit keep.
   The universe so vast a leap,
   it can always laugh, also weep.

The human soul on earth is captured,
   struggling all its earthly thwarted life
   for freedom to his domain of rapture
   awaiting his creator free from strife.

The many coloured faces on the board
   the different hearts of solid core
   with red blood pumping through,
   no matter what the colour,
   the heart is true.

The separate leaves grow on the trees
   all growth from the earth, one seed
   the branch from the trunk
   joins the leaves
   but the tree is all, in all in unity.

XXVI

THE WORLD HAS BEEN OPENED

It is the day when the door,
  Ever shut has been opened,
  The world at the core,
  With its knowledge and devotion,
  Now you can see the beauty
  Of the secrets of creation.

XXVII

THE SUN SPIRITUAL AND MATERIAL

What is this sun?
  Clothed with rays of life
  Scorching bursting the seed
  Developing the new tree,
  That gives air
  For man to breathe

What is this sun?
  Glorious with life,
  Bleeding, killing all and sundry
  Death to the lover
  Destruction to the beloved,
  Power almighty.

What is this sun?
  heart beat of all life
  Shaded behind the canopy,
  is the omnipotence, omnipresent,
  Power spirit of the soul divine,
  Sustainer of all life.

XXVIII

A CHANNEL FOR THE SPIRIT

Oh Poet, let the spirit flow
   Through the divine channel.
   Sing your song, let it grow
   As never ever heard
   On any television show.

XXIX

THE SOUL

We have discovered
  That we have a soul;
  Within that precious sign
  The spirit of life is held,
  Where all life unfolds divine.

XXX

THE FUNERAL

The soul, how can it escape?
  When the body is incapacitated
  From the stilled body.
  Which has now become cold.

This enigma, this soul,
  This harbinger of light,
  That real reflector, the sign
  Of the Creator's design.

This invisible immortality
  This unknowable might
  This life from which
  The power drives the light
  Through the body for all life.

XXXI

SPIRITUAL LIGHT

One's eyes are sore from the sun.
　That heat is like a wave
　Unable to see for the sun,
　Blinding life's glorious day.
　What is this wonderful cause
　Giving life, light for these days?

Gifts are made from glorious light,
　The source of light for this material
　world.
　The matured life is within.
　It is the sun of the heart
　The spiritual light that gives
　The smile, the thought, the love
　That strength to the world apart.

XXXII

THE HEALER

On this autumn evening, direct
    Beneath the surface, the seed is sown,
    From your balm within your heart,
    Your spirit, healing flows.

What a perfect eye, rests upon
    Shoulders, square and strong,
    To see you every day,
    Would keep the sickness away,
    To give balance, when all is astray.

XXXIII

KNOW YOUR SELF

Have you found yourself
    A nobler sign than majesty
    The star that shines within
    Loving heart's resplendency?

Under the core that lies,
    A heart of gold we say
    There is an untold wealth,
    Hidden within the clay.

From the heart will spring,
    A spark, a fire so bright
    That when the heart sings
    The room is flooded with light.

In that heart of gold
    Grows a selfless soul
    Who is the kindest person
    You have ever known.

XXXIV

FLIGHT OF THE SOUL

Oh, flight of the soul!
    Of soft feathers and fiery light.
    Your wings are strong,
    able and ready
    For your worldly flight.

You land like a soft breeze
    On the ground.
    Your steps like a dancer
    Gentle and sound.

Your stance firm and finer
    Than most creatures in life
    Your soul flies higher,
    The bird struggling with the light.

What is your aim?
    Through the wind and the rain.
    Climbing further to the unknown,
    Where you will discover your soul.

XXXV

TO BE AT ONE

Why do I try to write a word
    Make it scan and wish it heard
    Try to say what others said -
    Milton ,Yeats and Tennyson?
    Why do I try to weave a thread
    And make a picture in my head?

My task it seems to re-affirm
    Begin the story as of new
    For sage, apostle, kings and you
    To prove your thinking may
    come true.
What is it men wish to know?
    The universe in one is strung
    From the earth to the rising sun
    Where mushroom, dirt and eel sink
    Eel and worm and mole link.

When simple peasants sipped the wine
  Did yellow black and white incline
  To be the holy three divine?
  What Leonardo's brush has done
  And Wagner's mystic music spun
  have taught us all to be at one
  with unending spiral turn.
  Is this in life what we must learn?

XXXVI

NATURE'S MIRACLE

Elegance from the height to the ground
   You tower in splendourous form
   Shapes divine.
   Life nature moulded
   In such an intricate course;
   Oh tree! Spirit of majesty,
   Grown from a single seed.

Water from root to top
   Through veins of sap like tide
   Nourishment throughout.
   Height, grandeur, stature,
   Magnificent, in size.
   Oh tree! Heart of all mystery
   Grown from a single seed.

XXXVII

SPIRITUAL LIGHT

One's eyes are sore from the sun,
   Unable to see for the rays,
   That heat is like a wave
   Drowning ones sorrows away.
   What is this wonderful cause
   Giving light for these days.

Gifts are made from glorious light
   The source of light for this world.
   The matured life is within
   It is the sun of the heart,
   The spiritual light, that gives
   The smile, the thought, the love
   That strength to the world apart.

XXXVIII

A NEW REVELATION

As the dim lights fade
  And the shadows form,
  When the sun comes up
  We experience the dawn.

Love abides amongst the trees
  Seeping down in all the leaves
  Life awakens from its dormant state
  As from the dawn of the morn the
  sun escapes.

Every branch with life is filled
  As human kind, alight with love,
  is skilled.
  Through the heat the radiance comes
  The fiery atoms of the sun.

The heat is so strong, like a spiritual light.
  It affects all substance, brings new life,
  Gone from the body dead, and the
  mind asleep
  For all the human kind this radiance keep.

XXXIX

THE BEGINNING THAT HAS NO END

Victory unfurls its glorious wings
    Gliding down to the surface in spring
    The dark damp winter past
    Shadows of death withering
    Like the dried up grass.

The victory a shining sun
    The strong rays penetrating
    Through the thick undergrowth
    Awakens the smallest mole run
    To dance, the stretch in rhythm.

The grass its smallest roots,
    The strands stretch to the stream
    Seeking nourishment and moisture
    For the leaves ever verdant
    Continually remaining glossy green.

With life further bound
    Unfurling its studded crown
    Seeking, where can it be found
    That life that has a conscious
    Movement, a choice unseen
    That leads us to the beginning
    That has no end except the end
    Which starts the beginning scene.

XL

THE LIGHT OF JUSTICE

The light means understanding
   The knowledge that has come
   No more in the black pit
   Of ignorance
   Now we can see the sun.

The sun resembles Bahá'u'lláh
   Light, and love he brings
   From that wealth, heat
   We know evolution sings
   Of how life has sprung
   Towards the knowledge
   Of understanding love.

The outer man must
   Stand in the shade.
   And allow the sun
   With its glorious rays
   Strike the mirror
   Of the soul
   To see the God within.

And from that love,
   Justice was born
   What an exalted word
   Then put that word put into practice
   on this planet torn.

If Justice existed
   We could form a united plan.
   The Creator has given
   One pillar for reward.
   And one for punishment.
   Also in between
   for safety's sake
   He has given His bounty
   Of forgiveness to the sinner
   Through His grace.

XLI

SERVE THE CAUSE

O, Creator of love and might
  Send down upon us all thy light
  So that we may live and be
  As joyful and free as the breeze.

That we may be willing to serve
  And love your Cause as it deserves
  To whisper in every human heart
  The love thou hast wish to impart.

You have given
  Your image to humankind
  With a lamp to be ignited
  By the word of Bahá'u'lláh.

XLII

FATHER AND DAUGHTER

Father: It is the salty earth
    That gave you your body
    brought your birth
    Of beauty mixed with
    Love that had never
    Been set eyes upon
    Or felt within
    The distant wind.

Daughter: My body is often limp
    Sometimes feels weak
    It is my soul that
    Uplifts me in this life
    Long run of toil.
    Of sweat, all of strife.

XLIII

THE FIRST CAUSE

You are not my daughter
    If you cry,
    For your spirit must be
    High,
    When I will be executed
    My body die.

My spirit will be elevated
    Through grace,
    The greatest gift is
    To serve my Lord,
    Then love for the human race.

Be sure, father, I am
    your daughter.
    My step is in the same
    Hearth.
    But you must allow me
    To love you on your human path.

You have been chosen
    Only you, especially taken
    By our Lord
    As a sacrifice to His Cause.

XLIV

WHERE IS THE SOUL OF MAN?

Where is the soul of man?
Covered in the dust of the land
On the roof top or buried in sand
Where is the soul of man?

Where is the soul of man?
Floating around his body, grand
Or safe in the body, held in hand
Where is the soul of man?

Socrates and Jesus said,
The soul survives man when dead
If science were to clone a head
Would there be two souls, I dread?

At conception a soul is born
But when egg and cell meet
Is the same soul with the meat
Or do we have a soulless beast?

Where is the soul of man?
  A cloned body without a soul
  Drifting across allied fertile land
  Without a conscience whole.

What is the purpose of our fate
  Is it to build a family with a wife?
  To write a book on a tape
  Or grow the soul for the next life?